THE BIRMINGHAM SCRAPBOOK

VOL 1

Alton & Jo Douglas

Bull Street, c 1890. On the right you can see just one of the many spellings that "Birmingham" underwent throughout the years.

© 2005 Alton and Jo Douglas
ISBN 1 85858 274 1
Published by Brewin Books Ltd., Doric House, 56 Alcester Road, Studley, Warwickshire B80 7LG.
Printed by Warwick Printing Co. Ltd., Caswell Road, Leamington Spa CV31 1QD.
Layout by Alton and Jo Douglas

Ladypool Road, with Leamington Road on the left, Sparkbrook, 15th October 1959.

Front Cover: Queueing for Christmas dinners, Thorp Street, December 1936.

Contents

BREWIN BOOKS LTD

Doric House, 56 Alcester Road,
Studley, Warwickshire B80 7LG

Tel: 01527 854228 Fax: 01527 852746
Email: enquiries@brewinbooks.com

Vat Registration No. 705 0077 73

Dear Nostalgic,

I blame it on *Doctor Who!* The success of the BBC TV series has made me realise that looking at our books is a bit like a trip in the Tardis – travelling excitedly back through time (never forwards, of course, who wants to know what lies ahead). Take this book as a prime example – see the slums of the late 1800's, contrasting with some of the architectural splendour of turn-of-the-century Birmingham, marching men in the days of the Great War, the ups-and-downs of the 20's and 30's, the drama of 1939-45, wonderful images of the developing 50's and 60's, then on into the 70's and finally a brief tribute to Pebble Mill. A century of memories and even more faces than ever. So, go on, discover yourself and your past.

Yours, in friendship,

Alton

Aston Street, 1935

STATION SIRENS

*S*IR, — *Every evening the principal thoroughfares of the town swarm with the "ladies of the pavement." New Street, High Street, and Bull Street seem to be the favourite promenades, but the London and North-Western Railway Station is almost as attractive a resort.*

Surely they must select some more retired spot for the carrying on of their disgraceful traffic than New Street Station? No sooner does it begin to get dark than they begin to haunt the place, the platforms and bridge in particular.

Almost the first individual a young man fresh from the country observes on stepping out of the carriage is one of the frail sirens in question, and if he be liable to temptation, it is thus at once thrown in his way.

On the other hand ladies feel aggrieved that they are brought into contact with such social outcasts, and their husbands and brothers naturally wax indignant about it.

A Friend To Public Morality.
November 11, 1870.

Court No. 5, Thomas Street, c 1875. This was part of the Corporation Street development area.

BIRMINGHAM CRIMINALS AND THEIR HAUNTS.

THE LAST OF "THE GULLET."

Before the advance of civic improvement and commercial enterprise, the criminal haunts of Old Birmingham have gradually undergone a process of change or absorption, and have either altered their nature or been swept entirely away. There are now few vestiges of the notorious rookeries of 50 years ago. Some, however, still exist, but they are being lessened, and now by the erection of a large block of new business premises at the corner of James Watt and Stafford Streets, a remnant of the remarkable thoroughfare known as "The Gullet," has been removed. Little of it now remains but its evil reputation, and for the removal of this plague spot in the body social of Birmingham the city is indebted to its improvement scheme. When Alderman White went down it years ago, inspecting it for the information of the local authorities, the Gullet was a very unsavoury locality. For many previous years the street had been one of the lowest of the criminal haunts of Birmingham. Commencing in Coleshill Street, at the end of Stafford Street, it finished at the other end of Stafford Street, in Aston Street. Now Ryder Street forms the limit of the thoroughfare, and its continuance into Aston Street has been stopped, while the name of the shortened Gullet has been dignified into Ashley Passage. In days before the Improvement Scheme had been thought of the Gullet contained all the elements illustrating the lowest forms of human existence; not, of course, that all the residents were bad. Some were respectable, and the curious and often pathetic contrasts to be found in the Gullet and its vicinity afforded rich food for observation to the master-student of human nature.

The Gullet, again part of the rebuilding plans, 1875.

Workmens' cottages, Bournville, 1875.

New Street, c 1875. Three years later work began, at this point, to create Corporation Street.

Bournville Lane, 1880.

Moseley Village, 1880.

Cregoe Street School, 1880.

HORACE NICKSON,

High-class Cash Tailor,

305, BROAD STREET.

OPPOSITE NETTLEFOLD'S.

Scotch Tweed Suits, from **40/-**

Black Worsted Morning Coat, from **30/-**

All Wool Melton Overcoat, in any shade, from **30/-**

PURE SCOTCH TWEED TROUSERS FROM 13/-

The best workmen are kept on the premises, and all Goods are turned out in First-class Style.

SHOWELL'S

Dictionary of Birmingham.

A HISTORY AND GUIDE,

Arranged Alphabetically,

Containing Thousands of Dates and References to Matters of Interest connected with the Past and Present History of the Town— its Public Buildings, Chapels, Churches and Clubs—its Friendly Societies and Benevolent Associations, Philanthropic and Philosophical Institutions—its Colleges and Schools, Parks, Gardens, Theatres, and Places of Amusement—its Men of Worth and Noteworthy Men, Manufactures and Trades. Population, Rates, Statistics of progress, &c., &c.

Compiled by THOS. T. HARMAN, Author of "The Local Book of Dates," "Notes and Records," &c.,

FOR THE PROPRIETORS—

WALTER SHOWELL & SONS,

CROSS ✠ WELLS BREWERY, OLDBURY,

Head Offices: 157, GT. CHARLES STREET, BIRMINGHAM.

BIRMINGHAM:
Printed by J. G. Hammond & Co., 136-138 Edmund Street; and Published by CORNISH BROTHERS, NEW STREET.

Chamberlain Square, with the Central Library (left) and Mason College (centre) Ratcliff Place/Edmund Street, c 1880.

Camden Street School, Hockley, c 1887.

Hamstead Road Gate Lodge, Victoria Park, Handsworth, 1889.

Builders in Great King Street starting work on the Lucas factories, 1889.

Suffolk Street, c 1890.

Staff of the Birmingham City Hospital's Western Road branch, 1894.

Small Heath Harriers, before starting out on the Eight Mile Club Road Championship Run to their headquarters in Muntz Street, March 1899.

Ratcliff Place, with a cabbies' shelter in use, 1899.

Market Hall, Bull Ring, c 1900.

Corporation Street, from the Old Square, c 1900.

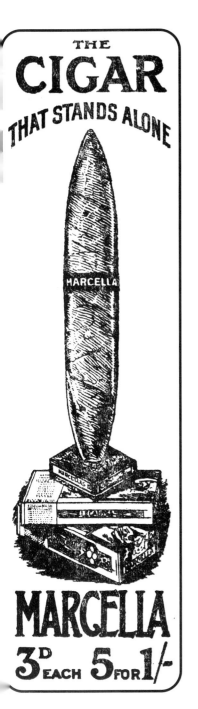

New Street, from Victoria Square, c 1900.

High Street, Aston, c 1900.

Handsworth Park, c 1900.

Birmingham Hospital for Women, Showell Green Lane,
Sparkhill, c 1900.

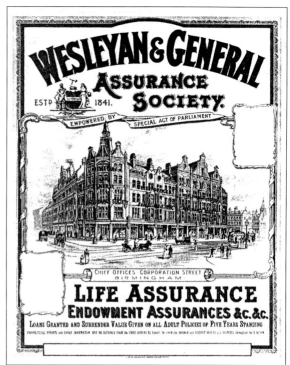

Fieldhouse Farm, Fieldhouse Road, Stechford, 1900.

East Birmingham and District Band of Hope Union.

SECOND CLASS

Certificate of Merit

Awarded to

Gertrude Ellen Bryan of Nechells Band of Hope,

for Report of Lecture by Mr. A. G. Bailey, F.T.I.

on

A Barrel of Beer.

October 1903.

President.
Chairman.
Secretary.

BIRMINGHAM CORPORATION TRAMWAYS

LORD MAYOR'S DISTRESS FUND

PLEASE GIVE FREELY

ALL YOU PAY FOR THIS CARD GOES TO THE FUND.

James Turner (wheelwright), Coventry Road, Hay Mills, c 1905. In 1913 the site was cleared and the Hay Mills and Yardley Picture House was erected. This was replaced, on an adjacent site, by the Adelphi in 1927.

Cadbury's first petrol-fuelled van, 1906.

Bournville Park, 1906.

City Arcade, 1906.

Steam Tram, Kings Heath, c 1906.

THE CHILDREN'S ENCYCLOPAEDIA

Birmingham University under construction, c 1907.

Maintenance men at Yardley Station, 1907.

The likely lads gather outside The Bull's Head, Coventry Road/Waterloo Road, Yardley, c 1907. The purpose of the get-together is long forgotten but someone thought it would be worthwhile displaying a bunch of flowers in a half-pint beer glass!

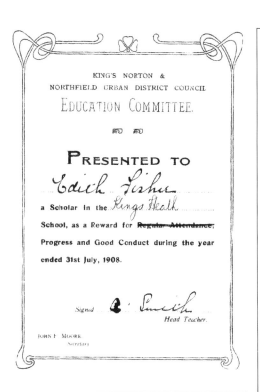

LADYWOOD ST MARGARET'S F.C. MCGREGOR CUP FINALISTS 1908-1909

Hay Mills Police Station, Coventry Road, 1909. This is now the Old Bill & Bull public house.

Birmingham University ready for business, 1909.

King Edward VII, Queen Alexandra and the Princess Victoria, leave the Council House to perform the official opening ceremony at Birmingham University, 1909.

1910

Harborne Fire Brigade, c 1910.

Birmingham Fire Brigade, c 1910.

Aston Fire Brigade, c 1910.

Small Heath Fire Brigade, 1910.

Green Lane, Small Heath, 1910.

Weaver's hairdressing saloon, Coventry Road, Hay Mills, May 1910.

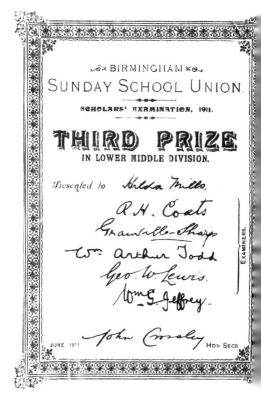

Happy Valley, Yardley Wood, 1911.

Leigh Road School, Alum Rock, 1911.

Ready for a day trip to Stratford-upon-Avon for the boys from Smith Street, Hockley, 1912.

Tucker Eyelets F.C., The Lad in the Lane, Aston, 1912.

Dudley Street, 1912.

The funeral of tram inspector, Thomas McLeod, killed by a runaway tram, Saltley, 1913.

Motor Cycles

WILEMAN,
145, HIGH STREET,
STIRCHLEY.

REPAIRS.

The Hill family, of Kings Heath, on an outing – to Yardley Wood! 1914.
We also know that the picnic food came from the Kings Heath grocer's
shop of Moyle and Adams.

The Ackrill family, from Bournville, arrive in Cheddar, Summer 1914.

Newbury's Ltd., Old Square, 1914. The store was bought by Lewis's, which closed in 1991.

ENGLAND'S · DECLARATION OF WAR AGAINST GERMANY.

Recruiting Parade, and the Pipe Band prepare to play, Victoria Square, 1914. The poster on the Town Hall proclaims, "We're both needed to serve the guns".

Recruiting Parade, Horse Fair, 1914.

BIRMINGHAM CITY BATTALION.

"FORWARD, BIRMINGHAM!"

Birmingham Volunteers' Territorial Army, Cannock Chase, 1914.

RALLY ROUND THE FLAG

EVERY FIT MAN WANTED

The first tank to be made at Metropolitan-Cammel Carriage & Wagon Co. Ltd., Washwood Heath, 1914.

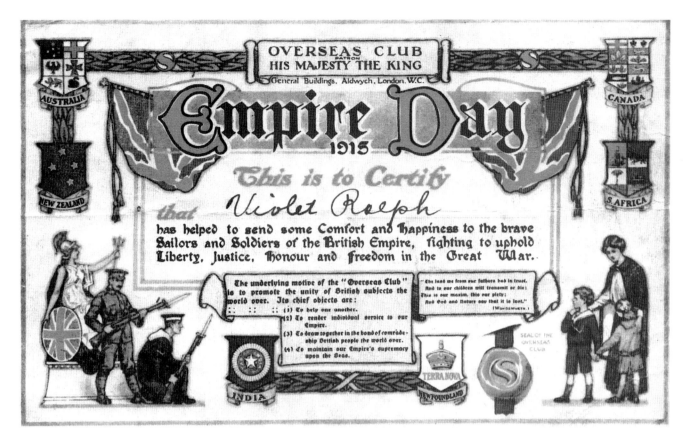

Empire Day certificate, 1915, for Violet Ralph, issued by the Overseas Club, His Majesty the King patron, General Buildings, Aldwych, London, W.C.

IMMEDIATE COMPULSION CERTAIN.

SINGLE MEN TO BE FETCHED.

The result of the all-important Cabinet meeting yesterday may be summed up as the triumph of "Single Men First." The cause for which we have fought for so many months and for upholding which we have been burnt by deluded members of the public and bombarded with fatuous abuse by the Hide-the-Truth Press has been won.

It was on May 21 that *The Daily Mail* opened its campaign by refusing Lord Kitchener's advertisement for recruits of forty. We refused that advertisement, as we then stated, because men of that age are almost without exception married, and because of the inefficiency, of the boundless cost, and last, but not least, of the inhumanity to wives and children of taking married men when single men remained by the million at their jobs. Now, at last, sane methods are to be introduced. The single men who have attested under Lord Derby's scheme are to be treated fairly. The married men are not to be betrayed. Immediate compulsion for those who have waited to be "fetched" is certain. Since they have not joined they will now be fetched.

District Nurses, Summer Hill Nurses' Home, Summer Hill, 1916.

Officers of the Balsall Heath and Bordesley Volunteer Training Corps., Holy Trinity Church, Camp Hill, 1916.

Convalescence at the First Southern General Hospital, 1917.

Birmingham University's Great Hall becomes the
First Southern General Hospital, 1917.

Wounded soldiers at Highbury Hall, 1917.

Staff at Highbury Hall, 1917.

A float in the "Win the War" Day procession leaves Kynoch's, Witton, 21st September 1918.

ARMISTICE ARRANGED
The Armistice was signed, before dawn on November 11, 1918, in Marshal Foch's special train in the forest of Compiègne

NCO's, C Co., 4th Battalion, Royal Warwickshire Regiment, Witton Barracks, 1918.

Chandos Road School, Sparkbrook, c 1918.

Amateur gardeners from the allotments in
Oxhill Road, Handsworth, c 1918.

Christ Church F.C., Summerfield Crescent, Edgbaston, 1918.

Local school children await the arrival of King George V and Queen Mary at Bournville, 21st May 1919.

The King acknowledges the greetings of local demobilised soldiers.

The King and Queen visit the Almshouses Quadrangle, Linden Road/Maryvale Road, Bournville.

Five Ways, from Harborne Road, 1920.

New Street, between Union Passage and Corporation Street, 1921.

Ernest Pinfold's shop, Coventry Road,
Hay Mills, 1920.

Bournville School, Linden Road, c 1920.

Addison Road, Kings Heath, c 1922.

Ansells' employees, Park Road, Aston, c 1923.

Ansells' annual display of vehicles, Cannon Hill Park, 1923.

TOWN HALL, BIRMINGHAM

Wednesday, Feb. 14th, 1923

BIRMINGHAM RAILWAYS CHORAL SOCIETIES

PROGRAMME

Entire proceeds in aid of Birmingham
**Children's Hospital, Cripples' Union
and Railway Benevolent Institution**

Proceeds of First Concert, at Town Hall
April 5th, 1922 — General Hospital £120
Railway Benevolent Institution - £40

PATRONS :

Sir John C. Holder, Bart., D.L.
Sir Charles Hyde, Bart.

Platform Decorations kindly supplied and arranged by City Parks' Department

Harold Saunders, Printer, 40 Gt. Charles St., Birmingham.

Junior Dept., Rookery Road School, Handsworth, 1923.

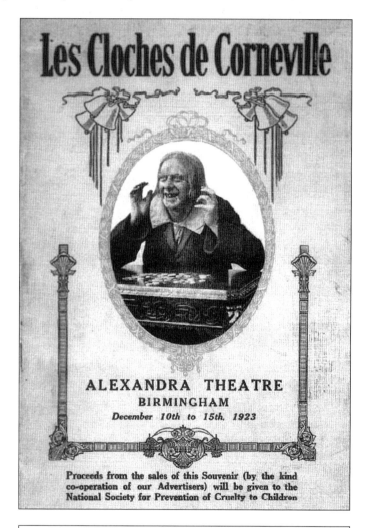

Les Cloches de Corneville

ALEXANDRA THEATRE
BIRMINGHAM
December 10th to 15th, 1923

Proceeds from the sales of this Souvenir (by the kind
co-operation of our Advertisers) will be given to the
National Society for Prevention of Cruelty to Children

THEATRE ROYAL
BIRMINGHAM

Lessees
THE THEATRE ROYAL
BIRMINGHAM LTD

Managing Director
Mr. PHILIP RODWAY.

Last Week of the Twice Nightly Season.

MONDAY, AUG. 25th, 1924,

For Six Nights at 6.40 and 8.50.

Direct from the CRITERION THEATRE, LONDON.

PERSONAL VISIT OF

BROMLEY CHALLENOR

and the ENTIRE LONDON COMPANY, including

ENID COOPER

IN

When Knights were Bold

"THREE ACTS OF JOY." THE FUNNIEST OF ALL FARCICAL COMEDIES.
By CHARLES MARLOW.

Moody Bros., Printers, 34, Livery Street, Birmingham

FOOTBALL AT VILLA PARK.
Under the auspices of the Aston Villa Football Club and
Birmingham & District Works Amateur Football Association.

Grand Charity Match for the Lord Mayor's Unemployment Fund

ASTON VILLA RESERVES

versus

WORKS ASSOCIATION

Thursday, December 27th.   **Kick-off 2.30.**

Admission 6d. No Tax.

The whole proceeds of this match are to be given to the Lord Mayor's Unemployment
Fund. A similar match last year helped us to raise a sum of £550 for this worthy
cause. Will you help us to raise this year at least £750 ?

Hon. Secretaries :—
J. H. WEBSTER, Birmingham & District Works Amateur Football Association.
G. B. RAMSAY, Aston Villa Football Club.

A. H. Meacham, Hay Mill Printing Works, Birmingham.—Tele. : Victoria 455.

Q 175

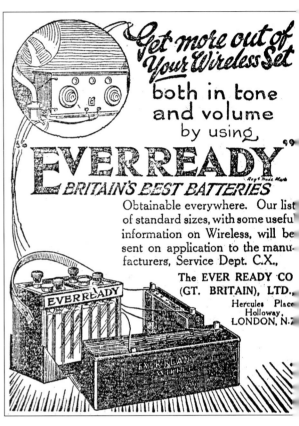

Kings Heath Junior Football Team, 1924.

Making car lamps, Joseph Lucas Ltd., Great King Street, c 1924.

Officers of the 5th Battalion, Royal Warwickshire Regiment, St Martin's, 1924.

Birmingham City Police Band, c 1925.

OCKER HILL WESLEYAN SUNDAY SCHOOL.

PROGRAMME OF CONCERT

BY THE

L.M. & S. Railway (BIRMINGHAM DISTRICT) Choral Society

On MONDAY, MARCH 22nd, 1926.

Conductor: MR. A. L. PROCTOR.   Accompanist: MR. FRANK HILL.

1—PART SONG	"A Spring Song"		Pinsuti.
2—SONG	"Rolling down to Rio"		
	Mr. Wilfred Bytheway.		
3—PIANOFORTE SOLO	Selected		
	Mr. Frank Hill.		
4—SONG	"I'll sing to you"		
	Miss Ethel Rose.		
5—VOCAL WALTZ	"A Night in May"		Dr. A. J. Silver.
6—VIOLIN SOLO	(a) "Melody in F"		Rubinstein.
	(b) "Sweet and Low"		
	Mr. Wilfred Proctor.		
7—TRIO	"The Knight and the Lady"		Schneizer
Accompanist: MISS PHYLIS MOSELEY (Prize Winner).			
	The 'Curlaw' Trio.		
8—SONG	"Love is a Slave"		Squire
	Miss Bessie Whitfield.		
9—PART SONG	"London Town"		German.

INTERVAL.

10—PART SONG	"In this hour of softened Splendour"		Pinsuti.
11—RECITATION	"The Portrait"		
	Miss D. L. Taylor.		
12—DUET	"Miserere Scene" (Il Trovatore)		Verdi
Mrs. P. Cathrall & Mr. J. Whitfield.			
13—SONG	Selected		
	Miss E. L. Phillips.		
14—MADRIGAL	"To take the air a bonny lass was walking"		Farmer.
PART SONG	"The Goslings"		Bridge.
15—VIOLIN SOLO	"In a Monastry Garden"		Ketelby
	Mr. Wilfred J. Proctor.		
16—SONG	"Land of Mine"		Jean Gilbert
	Mr. J. Whitfield.		
17—PART SONG	"Good-night, Beloved"		Pinsuti.

GOD SAVE THE KING.

Teaching staff from Alum Rock Road School, Ward End, 1926.

The opening of the West End Dance Hall, Suffolk Street, 1926.

37

Pigeon fanciers from the Rookery Road area of Handsworth, c 1928.

Raising money for the Birmingham Mail Christmas Tree Fund, The Cross Keys, (known to the regulars as "Watties"), Steward Street, Spring Hill, c 1928.

Members of Alfred Bird & Sons Ltd's concert party, Deritend, 1929.

40

1930

Warwickshire C.C.C. Second XI, c 1930.

The tornado strikes at Frazier Bros. Ltd. (grocers) Wordsworth Road/Coventry Road, Small Heath, 14th June 1931.

—— and at Green Lane.

The new Rotary Club boys' clubhouse, The Settlement, Summer Lane, October, 1932.

Empire's Fine Bill

The Empire, which has had a week "out," gets going again, Monday, with a slap-up vaudeville bill. At the head are those firm local (and universal) favourites, Ivor Moreton and Dave Kaye, popular "Tiger Rag" pianists from Harry Roy's band. Also at the head—for this is to be an honours-sharing week—is Nellie Wallace. Dave and Ivor will use two pianos in swinging gaily from one popular tune to another, always supported manfully by Ossie Noble, the whirlwind drummer. Nellie, one of our most brilliant low comediennes, will be—just Nellie Wallace. Among the funniest figures in her burlesque gallery is a wife of Henry VIII.

* * * *

Murray and Mooney return with their grand cross-talk act, in which Harry Mooney, interrupting his partner at every point of a thrilling recitation, retails a string of the wisest wisecracks imaginable. The Hickey Brothers and Alice appear in knockabout comedy, Marion and Irma in a symphony of motion, Joe Hastings and Shirley in a "vent" act, the Two Dancettes in stepped rhythm, Masu and Yuri in foot acrobatics, and Percy Val in tipsy tumbling.

Items

The Royal's new assistant manager, succeeding K. S. Frisby, is Charles F. Price, from the Gaumont-British organisation, which ultimately controls the house.

* * * *

The Repertory retains "1066 And All That." Capacity evening business is recorded.

* * * *

Twelfth night (January 7) will be marked at the Royal by the distribution, back-stage, of spiced cake and hot punch. Nita Croft and George Lacy will be hostess and host.

It was announced yesterday that at 24 October, 1932, the numbers of unemployed persons on the registers of Employment Exchanges in the Midland division were: 249,001 wholly unemployed, 102,998 temporarily stopped, and 502 normally in casual employment, making a total of 352,501.

This was 45,365 fewer than the number on the registers at 26 September, 1932, and 17,431 fewer than a year before.

The total on 24 October, 1932, comprised 287,254 men, 7,682 boys, 52,999 women and 4,566 girls.

Aston Lane railway bridge, 28th June 1933.

A day out from The Rose & Crown, Vincent Street, Balsall Heath, Summer, 1934.

Bennett Ashton and his Band, c 1934.

The Birmingham Post

AND JOURNAL

WEDNESDAY, OCTOBER 17, 1934.

Advertisements and all Business Communications should be addressed to The Manager, and letters dealing with Editorial Matters should be addressed to the Editor.

Head Office : 38, New St., Birmingham 2. Telephone Number (All Departments) : Midland 4461 (7 lines).

London : 88, Fleet St., E.C. 4. Tels. : Editorial, Central 8731. Commercial, Central 6180.

Wolverhampton : 72A, Darlington St. Tel. : 20817.

Walsall : 78, Bradford St. Tel. : 3453.

Coventry : 52, Hertford St. Tel. : 4708.

" The Birmingham Post " will be sent by post at the rate of One Shilling Weekly.

Hitler for Ever ?

Heil Hitler has served its turn—and served it very well. " Hitler for Ever " is to be the new slogan of Nazi Germany. And " ever " in this connection is to mean ever. It is to mean the whole life-time of the Leader who last August used one hand to grasp power as President without letting go, with the other, the power he had already taken as Chancellor. That is the only possible gloss to be put on the rather startling speech Dr. Lammers made yesterday in Berlin. And Dr. Lammers, as State Secretary for the Chancellor's office, ought to know the Hitler mind pretty well. In his view, which one may reasonably presume to be a reflection of the Leader's view, the Weimar Constitution is not only dead but buried. Hindenburg killed it, whether he meant to or not, when he installed Hitler as Chancellor. Hitler buries it now when, as Chancellor, he assumes a permanent Presidency. There was just one faint gleam of hope for democratic institutions in Germany while there remained of the Weimar Constitution the clause which provided for the election, once in seven years, of a President. A compact between President and Chancellor, even the develop-ment of a Pooh Bah Chancellor-President, was at least subject, under whatever disabilities that criticism might lie, to the criticism of a Presidential election. Even that check, it now appears, is to disappear. The Leader is President and Chancellor for life. No popular vote is to get rid of the Jekyll President—however Germany may come to dislike the Hyde Chancellor. It is an astonishing position for the citizens of a country that professes to enjoy free institutions. By a series of elections and plebiscites taken under duress, the whole elaborate system of democratic government has been used to establish a dictatorship.

The Green, High Street, Erdington, c 1935.

The Odeon, Birchfield Road, Perry Barr, 1935.

The parade to commemorate the Silver Jubilee of King George V and Queen Mary,
Colmore Row, May 1935.

Silver Jubilee party, New Canal Street, May 1935.

New Street/Corporation Street, c 1935.

Renovations at the Town Hall, 16th August 1935.

Chamberlain Square and the Museum and
Art Gallery, 1935.

An outing to the Lickey Hills from Cromwell Hall, Summer 1935

Acocks Green Junior School, 1935.

Richmond's pet food store, Alum Rock Road, c 1935.

What a peaceful view of Lichfield Road, Aston, taken in October, 1930. A young mother with her baby in a pram has all the time in the world to cross the road and there's plenty of room for cyclists as the occasional delivery van passes them by and a tram makes its way to Erdington.

FRAUD SUSPECT ESCAPES ARREST

Lib Dem candidate in postal votes probe flees to Pakistan

EXCLUSIVE

BY JEANETTE OLDHAM

POLICE officers who went to charge a Midland election candidate with forgery found he had left the country.

investigates electoral fraud in the region – in April, 2006, on suspicion of conspiracy to defraud the election process. Five other people were later arrested as part of the same inquiry.

It is understood that searches were

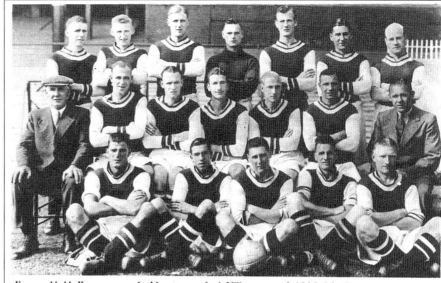

Jimmy McMullan managed this star-packed Villa team of 1935-36: Back row—Watkins, Gardner (England), Allen (England), Morton, Gibson (Scotland), Kingdon, McLuckie (Scotland). Middle row—Trainer Gooch, Waring (England), Astley (Wales), Brocklebank (England), Dix (England), Beresford (England), Manager McMullan (Scotland). Front row—Beeson, Broome (England), Houghton (England), Cunliffe (England), Blair (Scotland).

Aston Villa F.C., 1935/6.

Nine-year-old pupils at St Mark's School, King Edward's Road, Ladywood, 1936.

Covering the black case of the tennis balls with white felt, Dunlop's, 20th April 1936.

49

Budding thespians! St Paul's Church of England School, Vincent Street, Balsall Heath, 1937.

Prince's Suite, the New Inns Hotel, Holyhead Road, Handsworth, 1936.

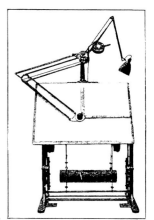

Temple Row, 2nd April 1937.

Coronation Day, The Rose & Crown, Vincent Street, Balsall Heath, 12th May 1937.

BOYS AND GIRLS IN DAILY ATTENDANCE
— AT —

LAWRENCE'S COLLEGE

36-42 CORPORATION STREET, BIRMINGHAM

The Largest, Best Equipped and Most Successful College in the Midlands.

Cherrywood Road Junior School, Winners of the Birmingham
Schools' Shield, Bordesley Green, 1937.

FREEDOM OF THE CITY
• •

At a special meeting of the City Council to be held on the 11th July, the Honorary Freedom of the City will be conferred upon Alderman Ernest Martineau, C.M.G., V.D., T.D., D.L., M.A., Alderman William Adlington Cadbury, Alderman Wilfred Byng Kenrick and Alderman Henry James Sayer, in recognition of their distinguished merit in the service of the city.

The formal resolution of the Council will be presented with the casket to each of the four members of the Council. The resolution to Alderman Martineau refers to his long service of thirty-six years as a member of the Council, to his service as Lord Mayor and Chairman of various Committees, to his grandfather and father who were also Mayors of Birmingham, and has also regard to Colonel Martineau's conspicuous service in the Auxiliary Forces of the Crown.

The resolution of the Council recording the eminent services of Alderman Cadbury refers to his long service as a member of the Council, as Lord Mayor and as Chairman of various Committees, and refers particularly to Alderman Cadbury's munificent gifts for the benefit of the city.

The resolution conferring the Freedom of the City upon Alderman Kenrick refers to his service as Lord Mayor, and particularly to his work as Chairman of the Education Committee, where his devotion and unsparing zeal have been of inestimable and lasting benefit to the youth of Birmingham.

Finally, the resolution referring to Alderman Sayer speaks also of his long service as a member of the Council, as Lord Mayor, as Chairman of various Committees and in his case has regard to Alderman Sayer's work on the Birmingham Tame and Rea District Drainage Board, as Trustee of very many charities and of his work for the hospitals.

Rehearsal for the Birmingham Charter Centenary Celebrations, Dyson Hall, 11th May 1938.

Pageant of Birmingham, Aston Park, 11th/16th July 1938.

In the shadow of The Prince of Wales Theatre, Broad Street, 1938

The Aston Hippodrome Orchestra rehearse, despite fire damage behind them, 18th February 1939.

Marlborough Road School children, evacuated to Worcester, being shown around Worcester Cathedral, 1939.

8th Battalion Royal Warwickshire Regiment, in camp at Arundel, 1939.

The President of the Law Society, J.T. Higgs, presents an address to the Lord Mayor, Ald. Theodore Pritchett, Council House, 31st January 1940.

Relaying the tram track outside the Civic Hall, Digbeth, 17th May 1940.

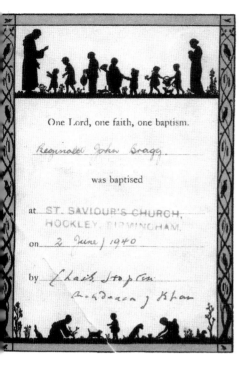

One Lord, one faith, one baptism.

Reginald John Bragg

was baptised

at ST. SAVIOUR'S CHURCH,
HOCKLEY, BIRMINGHAM.

on 2 June / 1940

by Chas Stopen
Archdeacon of Khan

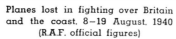

Planes lost in fighting over Britain and the coast, 8–19 August, 1940 (R.A.F. official figures)	German planes lost	British planes lost	British pilots safe
August 8	61	13	3
,, 9	1	—	—
,, 10	1	1	—
,, 11	65	26	2
,, 12	62	13	1
,, 13	78	13	10
,, 14	31	7	2
,, 15	180	34	17
,, 16	75	22	14
,, 17	1	—	—
,, 18	152	22	8
,, 19	4	—	—
TOTAL	711	156	57

TELEPHONE NORTHERN 1557.

The Birmingham General Cemetery
Co., Ltd.

E. H. MANNING, Registrar and Chaplain.

4 NOV 1940

FUNERAL CHARGES

for the interment of the late

	£	s.	d.
NEW	5	4	6
Re-opening Private Grave	2	9	0
Removing and Re-fixing Stone, &c.			
Elm Plank to protect Coffin ...		10	0
Special Time		5	0
Minister's Fee		5	0
Decorating Grave			
	£ 5	9	6

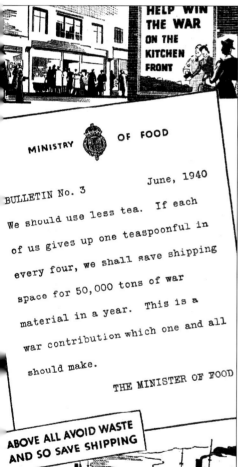

MINISTRY OF FOOD

BULLETIN No. 3   June, 1940

We should use less tea. If each of us gives up one teaspoonful in every four, we shall save shipping space for 50,000 tons of war material in a year. This is a war contribution which one and all should make.

THE MINISTER OF FOOD

ABOVE ALL AVOID WASTE AND SO SAVE SHIPPING

Birmingham mothers and children watch as an air raid shelter is being assembled, 1940.

Air Raid Precaution officers lining up for inspection, 1940.

Bomb damage in Slaney Street, off Steelhouse Lane, 28th October 1940.

Form 2B, George Dixon's Grammar School for Girls, City Road, Edgbaston, 1941. Note the shoulder straps for gas masks.

CITY OF BIRMINGHAM
AUXILIARY FIRE SERVICE

THIS IS TO CERTIFY THAT

A. D. WOOD.

HAS COMPLETED IN A
SATISFACTORY MANNER A
COURSE OF FIRE TRAINING

13th May 1941.

OFFICER COMMANDING THE
AUXILIARY FIRE SERVICE

Home Guard at Rednal Camp, 1942.

A decoy tank, made by the women of Dunlop's, c 1942. If you want to know how these were successfully deployed, during the Second World War, read the enthralling "The War Magician" by David Fisher.

The last tram travels along the Pershore Road, 5th July 1952.

American servicemen are shown around the body assembly shop at the Austin Motor Co. Ltd., Longbridge,
12th August 1953.

Regent Place, off Vittoria Street, Hockley, 1953.

Coronation decorations being put up in Sycamore Road, Aston, June 1953.

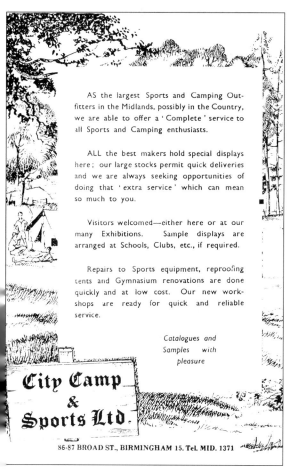

St Paul's Roman Catholic High School for Girls, Vernon Road, Edgbaston, 1955.

Degree Day Ceremony, The Great Hall, Birmingham University, 1955.

The Broadway cinema, Bristol Street/Wrexham Street, April 1955. It re-opened, after extensive alterations, in April 1956, as the Cinephone.

An outside toilet at 164/172 Clifford Street, Lozells, 1956.

Back houses at the rear of No 4 Graham Street, 1956.

West Boulevard, Quinton, 1956

Kingston Road, Bordesley, 8th May 1956.

Long Street/Kyrwicks Lane, Sparkbrook, 11th September 1956.

St Silas Mission Room, Wellesley Street/Nursery Road, Hockley, 1956.

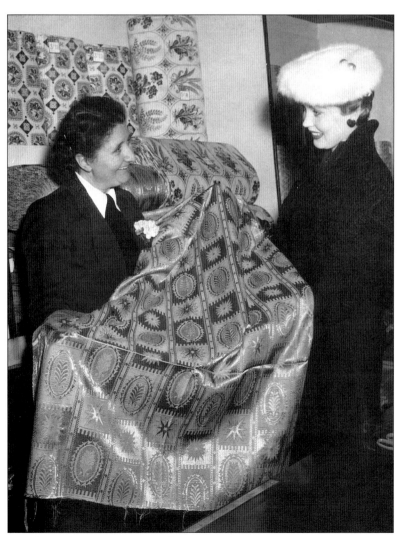

City-born film actress, Hazel Court, admires curtain material after opening the new Ten Acres and Stirchley Co-operative Society Ltd. store, Kings Heath, 6th October 1956. The assistant is Doris Goodwin.

Manchester United's goalkeeper, Ray Wood and Villa's Peter McParland, lie injured during the FA Cup Final, Wembley, 4th May 1957.

Stockfield Road, Acocks Green, 1957.

Eric Hollies leads the Warwickshire team out, against Surrey, in his last match, Edgbaston, 27th August 1957.

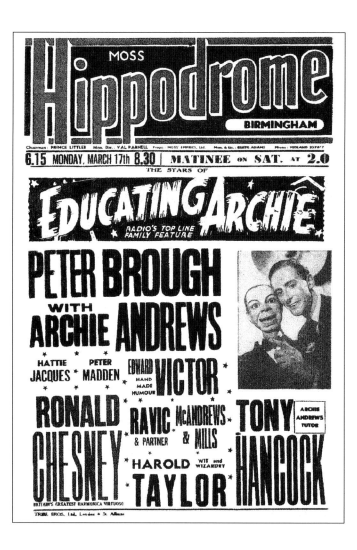

Actor, Robert Beatty, researching his role as a detective in the new ABC TV series, "Dial 999", visits Newton Street police headquarters, 16th June 1958.

Birmingham's Hedley Ward Trio, c 1959. Derek Franklin (left) was married to the actress, Beryl Reid.

Wholesale Market, Jamaica Row, c 1960.

BERNARD WITHERS

FLOWERS
FOR ALL
OCCASIONS

834 Alum Rock Road, B'ham, 8.
MEMBER OF TELEFLOWER SERVICE.
SPECIALISTS IN ALL HOUSE PLANTS

Monument Road, with Wood Street up on the left,
Ladywood 1960.

Percival Road Garage, Edgbaston, 25th May 1960.

All Night Jazz Festival at the Town Hall, 1960.

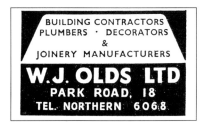

The Bell Inn and St Peter's Church, Old Church Road, Harborne, 27th April 1960.

Buck Street/Doe Street, 30th September 1960.

Haden Street/Arter Street, Balsall Heath, 14th December 1960.

High Street, with Hereford Square on the left, Saltley, 1961.

The Lord Mayor, Ald. Eric Mole, presents the Royal Life Saving Society's Affiliated Clubs' Challenge Shield to Bournville Youth Club, May 1961.

Regulars from the Bournbrook Tavern, Bristol Road, Selly Oak, 1961.

82

Scottish Dancing Team, Elkington Street School, Aston, c 1962.

Staff at A D Wimbush & Son Ltd., Alcester Road, Moseley,
1962.

Rear of Lupin Street, Nechells Green, 7th January 1963.

Joseph Lucas Ltd., Rugby Club 1st XV, 1963.

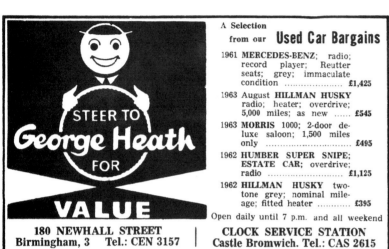

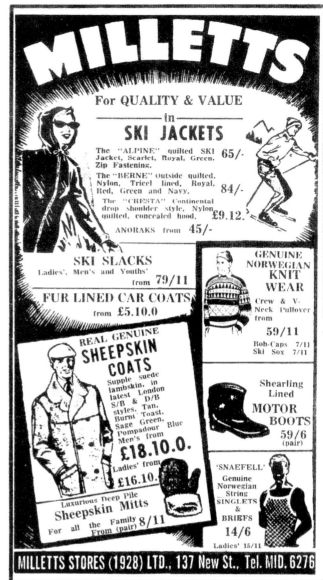

Edgbaston Reservoir, 30 July 1963.

Lunch in the new staff canteen, Woolworth's, Bull Ring, 25th September 1963.

Birmingham Co-Operative Society Butchers' F.C., current leaders in the Wednesday League, December 1963.

The Right Hon Leonard Cleaver, MP for Yardley, as part of his tour of constituency schools arrives at St Thomas More's Primary School, Horse Shoes Lane, Sheldon, 9th January 1964.

Some of the sixteen local beat groups that have formed themselves into the Offbeat Federation of Young Groups and Artistes, Navigation Inn, Tyburn Road, Erdington, 1964.

May Queen, Phillippa Clifford, and her Guard of Honour, Wychall Farm Infants' School, Northfield, 1964.

Television personality, Janice Nichols, is the guest of honour at the 18th birthday party of the Minors' Matinee, Palace Cinema, High Street, Erdington, 23rd May 1964.

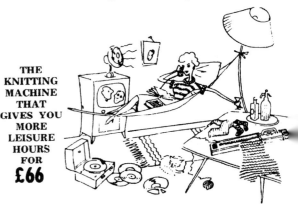

A court at the rear of High Park Street, Nechells Green, 1965.

The Lord Mayor, Ald. George Corbyn-Barrow and the Lady Mayoress, take part in the two-day religious ceremony at the Sikh Temple, Mary Street, Balsall Heath, 29th December 1965.

Church Road, Yardley, December 1965.

Swimming class, Yardley Wood Junior School, School Road, 1967.

Warwickshire cricketers admire the Gillette Cup pennant presented
to them at Edgbaston, 13th May 1967.

Elkington Primary School Football Team, 1967.

Rear of 64 Anderson Street, Ladywood, 24th June 1967.

Staniforth Street, off Corporation Street, 15th October 1969.

St Luke's Road, Highgate, 1969.

The City of Birmingham Lifeboat, 1970.

Young volunteers give up their Spring Bank Holiday to prepare a childrens' playground, Weoley Castle, 6th April 1970.

Floral farewell to the Minories

BIRMINGHAM shoppers are saying farewell to The Minories, as they have been known for generations, during the Spring Festival.

An the final memory of The Minories is as a Spring flower garden.

The wide public thoroughfare through Lewis's store is to be developed up to three storeys in a "close the gap" operation starting next month.

At ground level an arcade will still allow the public access.

"The Minories have been part of the Birmingham centre shopping scene for generations," said a Lewis's spokesman.

Sword swallowing

"We are sparing no expense in letting the area go out in fine style as our major contribution to Spring-time gaiety for the City Centre Festival."

More than £1,000 has been spent in converting the area into a flower garden, complete with gay sun shades, two rock pools, lawns, trees, shrubs and spring flowers.

Shoppers are now able to walk freely through this "instant garden." It was not there a few days ago and will disappear just as quickly after the Festival.

Then the building developers will start filling in the Minories.

Inside Lewis's a full programme of Festival attractions are taking place, covering a wide scope of interests.

On May 26, 27 and 28 there will even be a sword swallower, Stromboli, demonstrating his art in a Wilkinson Sword promotion.

Much of the fifth floor is being devoted to children's attractions, the highlight of which is a huge working model of an international airport.

The Queen arrives to open the Inner Ring Road, Colmore Row, 7th April 1970.

The Lord Mayor, Ald. Stanley Bleyer, receives a petition complaining about traffic hazards near Slade Primary School, Slade Road, Erdington, 17th June 1970.

Waiting to see Margot Bryant (Minnie Caldwell in "Coronation Street") at the opening of the new extension of Woolworth's store, High Street, Kings Heath, 18th October 1970.

The Annual Theatre Service with (left to right), Jean Bayliss, Freddie Davies and Anita Harris, St Philip's, 26th February 1971.

St Mary's Row, Moseley, 1971.

Choirboys line the stairs of the newly-decorated
St Philip's Cathedral at the Thanksgiving Service,
15th May 1971.

Hill Street/Paradise Street, 1971.

In the centre comedian, Les Dawson with, on his left, Pat Lancaster ("Robinson Crusoe") and Helen Garron, with Jack Tripp (right) the dame and three members of The Seekers, Alexandra Theatre, 8th December 1971.

Staff of Eddystone Radio Ltd., Alvechurch Road, West Heath, c 1972.

Still imposing, but becoming increasingly isolated, The Barton Arms holds centre stage, Aston, 2nd August 1972.

Carlisle Place, off Carlisle Street, Winston Green, 1972.

Something up at the deserted Marshall & Snelgrove building! New Street, 1974.

PEBBLE MILL

As a tribute to the now-defunct BBC broadcasting centre, we include a rare selection of some of the guests who appeared on the popular, "Saturday Night at the Mill", programme in the mid-70's. The centre officially closed on the 1st December 2004.

BBC tv

000052

invites you to

'*Saturday Night at the Mill*'

Doors open 10.15 pm	Saturday, December 18th, 1976
Commence 10.45 pm	**BROADCASTING CENTRE**
ADMIT ONE	**PEBBLE MILL ROAD**
(No children under 14 years)	**BIRMINGHAM**

Taken by the RAF, demonstrating photographic reconnaissance technique at high speed, Pebble Mill, c 1976.

Frankie Howerd

Natalie Wood and Robert Wagner.

Roger Whittaker, sings with the resident band of Kenny Ball.

Presenter, Bob Langley, dances with Ginger Rogers. If you look closely, on the left, you can see racing driver, James Hunt, playing trumpet with Kenny Ball's Band!

Back Cover: A view of Six Ways, Aston, taken from the new block of flats in James Street, 4th August 1966.

ACKNOWLEDGEMENTS

(for providing photographs, encouragement and numerous other favours)

Keith Ackrill; The late Stanley Arnold; Norman Bailey; Violet Baylis; John Birch; The Birmingham City Council Dept. of Planning and Architecture; The Birmingham Post and Mail Ltd.; The Birmingham Public Works Dept.; Diane Bloomer; Colin Bragg; Gordon Bunce; Carole Burton; Cadbury Schweppes Ltd.; Anne Cannell; Pauline Cartwright; Philip Haycock; John Hill; Doug Hobson; Shirley Houghton; Dave, Thelma and Tom Jones; Joyce Lockwood; Brian Matthews; Dennis Moore; Margaret and Ray Orme; George Peace; Colin Pinson; Bernard and Olive Poultney; Maurice Price; Jean Russell; Roy and Sheila Seabourne; Keith Shakespeare; Paul Southwick; University of Birmingham; Rosemary Wilkes; Brian and Freda Williams; Ken Windsor.

Please forgive any possible omissions. Every effort has been made to include all organisations and individuals in the book.

Unclaimed property, including over 100 bicycles, is up for auction at Victoria Road Police Station, Aston, 20th March 1958.